Everything You Never Want to Know About Hunting

Everything You Never Want to Know About Hunting

By BRUCE COCHRAN

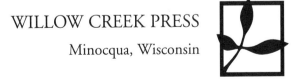

WILLOW CREEK PRESS

Minocqua, Wisconsin

ISBN 1-57223-034-7

Published by   WILLOW CREEK PRESS
                P.O. Box 147
                Minocqua, WI 54548

For information on other Willow Creek titles, write or call 1-800-850-WILD

Printed in the U.S.A.

For Babe and Max

Hollywood finally taps into the action potential of waterfowling with a new movie about ... you guessed IT — DUCK HUNTING!

Hunters will want to check out "Honey, I Shrunk The Bank Account," a new video featuring step-by-step instructions on how to explain to your wife why you bought that new $1,500 over-and-under when the house payment is overdue. Available from N-The-Doghouse Productions for $19.95.

Your male dog will be permanently cured of his tendency to urinate on everything once he tries it on the spark plug of your ATV while the motor is running.

When big bucks drop their antlers in the late winter, smaller bucks often pick them up and attach them to their own heads to impress does.

If you don't know where you are, consult your compass. If you don't know who you are, consult your hunting license.

If your hunting dog wants to sleep with you, don't worry about the smell. He'll get used to it.

The greenwing teal, our smallest, fastest duck, is said to be excellent table fare. If anyone ever actually hits one we'll know for sure.

Never take up reloading without first spending several hours in a casino to get your arm in shape.

Deer hunters who are fond of venison can avoid the back-breaking job of dragging a deer out of the woods by eating it on the spot.

Next time you find yourself in a crowded public hunting area on Opening Day, notice how many dogs are named "Dammit."

One of the hardest jobs a hunter ever faces is dragging a deer out of the woods ... especially when the deer doesn't want to go.

Before that first Javelina hunt, the prudent sportsman will make a few practice forays in the barnyard against TAME pigs to build his confidence

A dog training dummy stuffed inside your pants* will get you a lot of admiring glances in a singles bar.

* Be sure to put it in FRONT.

MTV has agreed to produce a hunter safety video to be called, "Yo, Dude! Don't Shoot Yo Mama!"

Buying your dog a bed with his name on it is a needless expense unless your dog can read.

Order your next 4wd with the "Bubba Package" — furry dice, tractor tires, highly visible gun rack, and rooftop deer clamps.

Canada geese mate for life, or at least until Mrs. Canada catches hubby fooling around with a hen shoveler.

Some states that offer primitive weapons hunts for archers and black powder enthusiasts are now taking the concept a step further — the VERY primitive weapons hunt.

Your hunting dog's digestive tract is one of the most amazing organs in nature. Somehow, it miraculously transforms 25 pounds of dog food into 225 pounds of poop every week.

You can prepare a youngster for duck hunting by making him sit in a cramped closet with nothing to do for several hours a day.

DON'T LET THIS HAPPEN TO YOU!
Bob was walking back to camp at dusk.
He was out of ammo and his clothes
were soaked with doe-in-heat scent.
Then it happened ...

On the theory, "if they'll watch golf they'll watch anything," television executives now have plans to televise deer hunting.

You can give your retriever a daily workout by sending him for the morning newspaper. You can teach him multiple retrieves and add some excitement to a dull morning by sending him for the neighbors' papers as well.

A hunting invitation to a young man often meets with opposition from his wife. Invite an older man, however, and the opposite will usually occur.

When you enter a crowded small-town cafe for a pre-dawn breakfast during hunting season, leave one man awake in case the food arrives.

Spring turkey hunters will love the new wild-flower camo patterns. Available in buttercup, fairy slipper and evening primrose.

If you get lost while archery hunting, fire three shots in the air to notify potential rescuers of your location.

There are certain ways to tell when you've been away from home on a hunting trip for too long.

Obese duck hunters can expand their comfort zone by utilizing a product originally designed with the ladies in mind — maternity chest waders.

Tired of hearing your wife complain about the money you spend on hunting equipment? Try wearing your $90 shooting ear muffs around the house.

Somewhere in America a new camouflage pattern is developed every 30 seconds.

Experienced turkey hunters know the droppings of a gobbler from their being shaped like the letter "J." Some very literate and agile gobblers have been known to spell their names.

Never scold your retriever for bringing things to you in the off-season. He is only responding to those many hours of training you put in with him when he was a pup.

Except for occasional flirtations with impressionism, wildlife painters have never embraced any of the historically important movements of the art world. Vast new horizons await the first artist brave enough to venture from the accepted wildlife genre.

THE GOOD NEWS IS, WE HAD A RECORD DEER HARVEST OF 165,792. THE BAD NEWS IS, IT WAS ALL BY ONE GUY.

Conservation agents in some areas estimate that the illegal deer kill equals or even exceeds that of legitimate licensed hunters who play by the rules.

You know you're definitely in big cat country when you encounter an enormous sand box.

Can't seem to bag a buck? You may be using a scent that has been recalled to the factory. Over 10,000 "Doe-In-Heat Scent" Bottles were mistakenly filled with "Doe-Who-Couldn't-Care-Less Scent."

The familiar "V's" of waterfowl in flight are the result of years of evolution. Early ducks started with the letter "A" and worked their way through the alphabet until they hit upon a successful pattern.

Geese that live on golf courses can be successfully hunted during the moulting season. A driver is recommended for the giant Canadas, a five iron for the smaller subspecies.

ATTENTION BALD HEADED TURKEY HUNTERS! Make a fashion statement while displaying your trophies! Have your gobblers' beards surgically implanted in your scalp.

Waterfowl hunters estimate that, by the year 2000, the various licenses, stamps, permits and special regulations will outweigh the typical bag of decoys.

Proud (or not-so-proud) parents are now sporting bumper stickers touting their kids' accomplishments in the field.

The question has baffled man down through the ages: how do waterfowl navigate on their long migration flights? But nature poses questions for all of us, even for the ducks.

You and your hunting dog will develop a closer working relationship in the field if he is treated like a member of the family during the off-season.

On his first few trips afield, a young dog will sometimes point non-game birds. You can discourage this behavior by shouting and jumping up and down.

Frequent use of ROBO BUCK, the mechanical deer used by conservation agents to snag poachers, is having an unintended effect on the breeding habits of some whitetail populations.

Tchaikovsky's 1812 Overture, cranked to the max on a portable boombox, will often entice reluctant turkeys to gobble.

When hunting out West, if you encounter a speedy, goat-like animal with horns on its head, it's a pronghorn. If the horns are on the other end, it's a wronghorn.

Hunters who attend church regularly throughout the rest of the year need not feel guilty about hunting on Sunday mornings. A brief, informal worship service can be held almost anywhere.

While deer are noted for their wariness and keen sense of smell, their bizarre sense of humor has gone largely unnoticed.

To counteract the deer's phenomenal sense of smell, many hunters refrain from using soaps, colognes, lotions, etc., before hunting. Others, however, question the effectiveness of these tactics

The ring-necked pheasant was introduced into this country in the 1800s. It was chosen over its cousin, the ring-RUMPED pheasant, because wildlife experts feared the highly visible white ring on the latter's hindquarters would present too easy a target for hunters.

Hunters who have graduated from sensitivity training can continue to enjoy the use of firearms while appeasing their new age friends by fitting their rifle scopes with the new peace reticle.

When big game hunting, keep in mind that only a very large, high-ceilinged room can accommodate the mounted head of a major trophy such as elk or moose.

COCHRAN!

Sandhill crane hunters have long prized this big, graceful bird as table fare. The drumstick alone feeds four people and the bone can be used as a tomato stake.

Hunters who live in small apartments and lack a proper "trophy room" in which to display large animal heads should confine their trophy mounts to smaller species.

As the popularity of outdoor sports increases, hunting shows will spread to the major television networks and in no time at all we'll be seeing scenes like this ...

Taking a tip from fisheries biologists who have set aside certain waters as "fly only areas," some field trial clubs now feature "fleas only areas."

In areas where the whitetail and mule deer range overlaps, there is mounting evidence that the larger mulies do not always get along with their smaller cousins.

When fall approaches, confident bowhunters who welcome a challenge eagerly anticipate the ultimate test of skill — ARCHERY TEAL SEASON.

Products that claim to "control fleas" do not actually eliminate them. They merely teach them to march in unison on your dog's body.

No one has ever seen a coot fly more than 20 or 30 yards. It is believed they migrate by walking or possibly hitchhiking.

Never clean your glasses with the same hand-kerchief you blow your nose on.

The feathers of a bird you intend to mount can be protected by stuffing it into a pair of women's panty hose. Be sure the woman is not wearing them at the time.

Turkey hunters love the sound of a good friction call. However, no reliable study has ever documented how it sounds to a turkey.

When your veterinarian tells you to bring a stool to the office, he's not suggesting that his waiting room has a shortage of seats.

Start your young retriever off on small birds such as teal and work up to larger game. A lightly wounded goose can be quite intimidating to a pup.

The laptop computer has enabled outdoor writers to actually experience exciting wilderness adventures and write about them at the same time.

During the peak of the rutting season, an extremely active buck leaves a telltale track that can be easily followed.

Farm boys whose early amorous adventures involved sheep should be wary of continuing this practice with the bighorn.

When the game warden says he wants to check your bag, never drop your pants.

Homeless people who live in dumpsters often make excellent duck hunters because they are used to spending hours in cramped, smelly places with nothing to do.

Never ask permission to hunt when a pheasant opens the farm house door.

When told to "sign your duck stamp across the face," an estimated 30 percent of hunters misinterpret these simple instructions.

Bluebills banded in Alberta often wind up in a marsh in Louisiana. Mallards banded in Saskatchewan often wind up in a crock pot in Kansas City.

While it is good manners to offer a token of appreciation to farmers who allow hunting, such gifts should be chosen with great care.

Deer decoys are becoming popular with hunters. But whether they will ever achieve the same popularity with collectors remains doubtful.

In addition to the standard duck and goose calls, the well-equipped waterfowler won't venture into the marsh without his pintail whistle, wood duck squealer, and other assorted noisemakers.

If your Labrador bitch is bred by the St. Bernard next door, do not despair. She may present you with retriever pups who can fetch you a drink.

The biggest bucks usually choose the biggest trees on which to rub. If you find a rub on a telephone pole, call your taxidermist and take cover at once.

The Second Amendment guarantees your right to keep and bear arms. It does not, however, guarantee your right to keep and arm bears.

The use of scents and tree stands are standard deer hunting techniques. However, recent studies indicate that some deer hunters are starting to wise up.

The single hunter in search of a mate who shares his passion for the sport should be on the lookout for women who wear choke tubes for earrings.

ATTENTION DEER HUNTERS!

Why pay for commercially-bottled raccoon urine to mask your scent when you can collect your own with **TREE PEE**, the tree-mounted animal urinal? Mounting screws and collection bottle included.

ATTENTION DUCK HUNTERS!

Why fight the dark? Get BUGGER BEAM, the tiny flashlight you insert in your nose, leaving both hands free to set out decoys or load up for that first flight.

Duck calling contests are judged by a so-called panel of experts who may or may not know good calling when they hear it. A true test of successful calling can only be judged by the REAL experts — DUCKS!

Don't be surprised if, in order to conform to the latest trends in feminine footwear, your teenage daughter commandeers your favorite pair of hunting boots.

Taking a cue from the waterfowling fraternity, many successful deer hunters are now using decoys. NOTE — Some modifications in tactics may be necessary.

Young retrievers often make mistakes that would disqualify them in a field trial. But as long as your dog is eager to please you should overlook his minor stylistic blunders.

There's no need for bench rests and other sissified gadgets when you sight-in your deer rifle using the "Bubba Method." Just toss a beer can into the creek and fire a few rounds at it as it floats away. If the bullets strike within a yard of the can, you're ready.

While the Indians utilized nearly every part of the buffalo they killed, they were never into trophy hunting for obvious reasons.

Your upland game dog need not hit a classic point like the dogs in the old sporting prints. As long as he somehow lets you know he's found birds he's doing his job.

By paying careful attention to the chart below you can butcher your deer using only a chainsaw.

Turkey hunters who use camo makeup should never refuse advice from their wives or girl-friends. After all, the gals have been using make-up for years.

Hunters who wear false teeth can often call bucks into range by rattling their dentures against their rifle barrels.

Never go hunting with a man who won't eat biscuits and gravy.

If you dog is too hard-headed for an electric collar, try a nuclear collar. Available from BLAST-A-BITCH in blaze orange or camo

In the old days hunters often came from rural backgrounds and could repay their host for a day's hunt by helping out around the farm. Today, however, most hunters are city-bred and farmers are more likely to let them hunt if they promise NOT to help.

Cockleburs can be removed from the coat of a long-haired dog by pulling him rapidly through the jaws of a large northern pike

Any big headstrong retriever will occasionally rebel. When this happens, take him to his crate or kennel and leave him there until his attitude changes.

The market hunter, long maligned for his wanton overharvest of waterfowl years ago, was actually ahead of his time. After all, those punt guns were loaded with STEEL bolts, nuts and chains.

Inscriptions carved into the walls of caves by early man indicate that ownership of weapons has always been a touchy subject.

You can lengthen the working life of your retriever by fitting your blind with whatever equipment is necessary for him to enter the water easily.

Tattoos are becoming popular among people who would not have dreamed of having one several years ago. Will this trend extend to the outdoor community?

If you consistently miss birds, try patterning your shotgun. You may come up with an explanation.

Never wear your hunting garb into town. Publicity about militias have given camouflage a bad name.

Silicone breast implants, available from your local medical supply company, are better than sand bags for steadying your rifle during sight-in sessions.

The whitetail deer has proved to be amazingly adaptable to man and is frequently sighted in urban areas.

Next time you have an intestinal disorder take a tip from your hunting dog. Drag your butt across the rug and whimper.

A painting of a gadwall foot stuffed into an empty shotgun shell will never win the federal duck stamp contest.

Only an immoral man with no conscience can blame his own intestinal indiscretions on his faithful hunting companion without the slightest tinge of guilt.

Tell a Navy man that you "shot a deer in the head" and his perception of your statement may not be entirely accurate.

Next year, a popular outdoor magazine will unveil its first swimsuit issue featuring truck stop waitresses in camo and blaze orange bikinis posed against a cornfield backdrop.

Outdoor rappers HWA (Hunters With Attitude) have released a new rap song that deals graphically with field dressing game. Sample lyrics: "Cover th' eyes of th' kids and wife. They won't believe where you stick yo' knife."

With the popularity of deer decoys on the rise, can the use of blocks in pursuit of other big game be far behind?

If you know someone who has a relative who once dropped a kernel of corn on the ground in a state where you have hunted during the past ten years, you are probably guilty of baiting.

While we view the familiar flight pattern of migrating geese as a "V," the Romans saw it quite differently.

Something you'll never see on "Celebrity Outdoors."

If you keep seeing the same duck fly past your blind it is probably lost and flying in a circle.

Hunters who suffer from indigestion will welcome the new BELCH RIGHT NAVEL STRIP. When placed over your navel this adhesive strip helps open abdominal passages and restore proper belching.

Now we know the answer to that age-old question that has bewildered art historians down through the ages — "Why was the Mona Lisa smiling?"

When tracking a deer, keep in mind that your quarry will eventually bed down in a warm, dry place.

Yₒu can make the off-season go by more quickly by watching hunting videos. Your wife, who always has your best interests at heart, will gladly give up watching her favorite soaps and sitcoms to join you.

No matter how strong the bond between you and your retriever, you never really know what's going on inside his brain.

Never take your firearms to a gunsmith who refers to parts as do-hickies and thing-a-ma-jigs.

You cannot substitute a Marilyn Monroe stamp for the federal duck stamp, even though it's more fun to lick.

Anthropologists believe the shooting sports were preceded by the throwing sports.

Several presidents have been avid duck hunters, beginning with George Washington. However, one mystery remains: if he couldn't tell a lie, how could he have been a duck hunter?

If you're going to put boots and a vest on your bird dog, why not go all the way?

Turkey hunters who have clamored for tighter and tighter choke restrictions will love "CHOKE THIS!!", a radical new choke tube that forces the pellets out of the muzzle in a single file.

Pay special attention to your diet as hunting season approaches. Early morning intestinal problems can play havoc with your duck calling.

You can break the disgusting habit of picking your nose by wearing an empty shot shell on each finger.

The predictability of the mainstream outdoor press has become ... well, predictable. Some suggestions for livening up the format appear above.

Those long hours in the car on your family vacation are an ideal time to practice your duck and goose calling. You will notice a dramatic improvement in your hunting success and your family will enjoy it.

Don't be discouraged when you find attractive hunting land posted. The landowner may have had an unpleasant experience with slob hunters but will possibly allow you on his property if you are courteous and polite.